Success in Dependency Court
A Parent's Guide to Dealing with CPS

Success in Dependency Court
A Parent's Guide to Dealing with CPS

Nancee E. Tomlinson

2022

Original Copyright © 2016 by Nancee E. Tomlinson
Print Publication © 2017 by Nancee E. Tomlinson
Second Publication © 2018 by Nancee Tomlinson
Third Publication © 2020 by Nancee E. Tomlinson
Fourth Publication©2021 by Nancee E. Tomlinson
Fifth Publication©2022 by Nancee E. Tomlinson

All rights reserved. This book or any portion thereof may not be reproduced or used in any manner whatsoever without the express written permission of the publisher except for the use of brief quotations in a book review or scholarly journal.

First Printing: 2016
Second Printing: 2017
Third Printing: 2018
Fourth Printing: 2020
Fifth Printing: 2021
Sixth Printing: 2022

Nancee Tomlinson
P.O. Box 102
Athens, Georgia 30603
www.tomlinson-lawfirm.com

DISCLAIMER: The general advice provided in this book does not address any particular case or provide specific advice on any particular case. Readers should always consult an attorney to represent their specific interests and the specific facts of their case.

Cover photo: © 2022 Nancee Tomlinson
Author photo: © 2014 Braxton Barden

Table of Contents

Introduction..7

Section I: Rights of Parents..9

Section II: Working the Case Plan..............................17

Chapter 1: Learn the System..19

Chapter 2: Succeed with Truth......................................21

Chapter 3: Trust Issues..23

Chapter 4: One Step at a Time......................................25

Chapter 5: Priorities..27

Chapter 6: Different Expectations................................29

Chapter 7: Calendar Control 31

Chapter 8: Be the Bigger Person..................................33

Chapter 9: What's Important..35

Chapter 10: Show Commitment..................................37

Chapter 11: Choices..39

Chapter 12: When CPS Errs..41

Chapter 13: Keep Asking...43

Chapter 14: Make the Most of Time...........................45

Chapter 15: Record Keeping.......................................47

Chapter 16: Monetary Support...................................49

Chapter 17: Employment 51

Chapter 18: Family Tree 53

Chapter 19: Attitude 55

Chapter 20: Tests 57

Chapter 21: Paternity is NOT Magic...........................59

Chapter 22: Cast of Characters 61

Chapter 23: Always Ask for a Lawyer..........................63

Chapter 24: Disagreement with Diagnosis.....................65

Chapter 25: Drug Testing..67

Chapter 26: Fair Game..69

Chapter 27: Requirements 71

Chapter 28: Source of Change....................................73

Conclusion...75

Quick Reference 76

Section III: Words, Phrases, and Definitions..............79

Section IV: Record Keeping..................................89

Tracking Your Case Plan..91

Names, Numbers, and Titles......................................95

Contact Log...98

Court Dates...131

Introduction

The most difficult moment in a CPS case happens when the judge decides that the child or children must stay in State custody. Too many parents spend fruitless time and energy fighting that decision, battling with CPS, praying that their children will be coming home.

A parent's inability to move beyond the hurt and pain of CPS's taking custody of their child is the most significant barrier to getting children home that I have observed.

What happens after the judge's decision can determine whether you, the parents, bring your children home.

Parents must set aside their anger, worry, fear, and disappointment. In that moment, you should shift aside the hard feelings toward CPS and start to focus on the steps to complete the case plan and regain custody. There may also be some discomfort with or hard feelings toward the judge who makes the decisions in the case; these too can be barriers to your regaining custody. Ultimately, the judge will make the decisions on the case and parents must find a way to let go of that anger. Begin with the goals of the case plan. Learning the other rules, necessary shifts and changes in behavior, and the social rules expected by professionals will help.

As a practicing attorney, I have realized that my clients frequently did not comprehend how to survive the CPS case plan process. Many clients do not understand that interacting with the Court and CPS is different from day-to-day interactions with social groups and family. Working with CPS is hard when the rules for accomplishing the goal differ from the rules you use routinely; harder still when you do not *understand* that the rules are different.

After years of observing parents mishandling this

transition from fighting to cooperating, I've written this book to aid parents in the transition and to help them understand that working the case plan and dealing with CPS politely brings children home faster in most cases.

Many times, parents did not understand the unwritten rules, the rules of social conduct that apply outside their circle of friends and their family groups. The rules that apply in a courtroom also apply in working with the professionals at CPS and the service providers sent by CPS.

Changing a negative attitude toward CPS may be the hardest step to take. **Parents facing dependency cases can find themselves and their children trapped in a cycle with a state's child custody department.** Follow the advice in this booklet and the necessary change in attitude might be easier, and the benefits will be significant.

The steps explained in the following pages provide a framework to help you work with CPS and regain custody of your child. This advice requires **action** and **change** from parents. The action and change will help you get your child home. Like advice for any difficult task, the steps set forth in this book will have to be used repeatedly. The goal to obtain custody will not be achieved overnight. This challenge could, in fact, last months. Parents must be ready to do what is necessary to regain custody of their children and get CPS out of their lives once and for all.

Section One

Rights of Parents

Know Your Rights as a Parent in a CPS/DFCS Case

When a child is in foster care, parents do retain certain rights, but these rights are primarily in the area of objecting to decisions made by CPS and/or foster parents. However, be aware that if the parent does object, the court is the ultimate decision maker. Simply objecting does not require change in plan. If the parent and CPS cannot reach an agreement, then the matter will be put before the judge.

Parents should be mindful to take great care with objections and not object to every little thing. Decisions will be made for your child and your child's wellbeing. Inserting yourself into every decision may create unnecessary hostility and make it even harder to achieve what you want.

Right to Attorney at All Stages Beyond Immediate Removal

Always, always, always request an attorney. You should request an attorney to help navigate the Court processes. Attorneys understand the Court rules and the requirements that CPS must follow.

The attorney cannot complete the case plan for you. If a crisis arises, however, the attorney can help you ask the judge for changes. Keep your attorney up to date on what is happening in your case. Given time to prepare, an attorney can advocate for you around issues that are important to you and find witnesses when appropriate.

Right to Fight Dependency Petitions

A parent always has the right to fight a dependency petition by DFCS or a private dependency petition. In some cases, fighting is a good decision. In other cases, though, fighting might not be the best choice. Consult your attorney. Listen and talk about the reasons to fight and the reasons to consent. Ultimately, it is the parent's decision, but get your attorney's advice.

Right to a Hearing on Protective Order

When DFCS asks for a Protective Order from the Court, a parent can fight that order. Again, consult with your attorney. Sometimes to avoid taking a child into DFCS custody, DFCS will ask for a Protective Order. Consider your options before making a rash decision at this stage.

Right to Object to Out-of-State Vacations

Foster parents may choose to take a foster child on vacation. This practice is generally permitted and oftentimes beneficial for a child. Under some circumstances, a vacation whether in-state or out-of-state, might interfere with scheduled visits or medical/mental health appointments.

Parents may object to vacations out of state because the child will be taken outside the jurisdiction of the Court. Before you enter an objection to a vacation for your child, consider the reason you object. What is best for the child in this particular circumstance? *If not going on the trip is best for your child, then objecting may be appropriate after consultation with your attorney.*

Right to Participate in Medical Decisions

When children enter foster care, parents maintain the right to participate in the medical decisions concerning the child. If DFCS, foster parents, and parents disagree about a non-emergency medical decision, that issue might require a hearing for the judge to decide what's best. Immunizations in particular may raise a conflict between parental choice and a policy at DFCS. It is important to note that some religious beliefs must be honored by DFCS and the State. Those religious preferences must be genuine and presented to DFCS and the State in order that the preferences can be considered in the decision-making process.

Discuss medical matters or issues with your attorney in order that the issue may be properly brought before the Court.

Right to Be Present for Medical Appointments

As stated earlier, parents retain the right to be involved in their child's treatment for medical issues, unless the Court specifically forbids their participation. Parents should and do have the right to be notified of scheduled medical appointments. Being there for your child and participating shows that you are working to maintain that parent-child bond. Being involved and being aware of a child's treatment shows the judge that you want to improve and change.

Right to Visit Child

Parents have the right to visit their child in foster care. But there are some circumstances which will prevent visitation. Allegations of physical abuse and/or psychological abuse are examples. Normally, parents may visit. These visits may be supervised in the beginning. Understand that the supervision not only protects ~~not only~~ the child but also protects you. The supervisor's report of how you act and participate can make the difference between ongoing foster care lasting for weeks and having it last for months. Showing the supervisor your ability to parent and properly discipline a child helps a judge understand your abilities and capacity to parent, because the judge will get a report from the supervisor, who will be an independent, unrelated person.

Most importantly, visits support the parent-child bond, which must exist for a child to be comfortable and safe with a parent.

Right To Be Heard by Judge on Any Issue in a Case Plan

DFCS will propose a Case Plan. This Case Plan is usually adopted by the Court without much input from anyone beyond DFCS. You, through your attorney, should ask to review the Case Plan ahead of time and five (5) days' notice. If something in the proposed case plan does not make sense, ask about it in court. Your attorney can ask the case manager why this specific step is included. Understanding the reason for a step in the Case Plan will help you understand why it's important.

On the flip side, Case Managers sometimes throw in steps because "it's what we always have put in." Case plans are not "one size fits all." Ask, <u>through your lawyer</u>, about steps that don't seem to apply to your case. Ask the judge to remove any unnecessary barriers to reuniting with your child.

Right To Be Heard by Judge on Changes in Case Plan If DFCS Won't Adjust

A Case Plan can be burdensome. There are many tasks to accomplish, and you may not think that there is enough time to complete the Case Plan, work, and visit with your child. If you're having difficulty with DFCS, talk to your attorney. Raise the issue when you go to court for a review. Or ask, <u>through your attorney</u>, for a hearing on the issue.

Judges understand the burdens on parents. DFCS sometimes just can't quite understand. Instead of giving up on the Case Plan, take it to the judge for a decision about what needs to be happening.

Right To Be Heard by Judge on Issues with DFCS

If you feel DFCS isn't meeting the obligations of the case plan, that the referrals for services are taking too long, that no one calls you back, that nothing is happening in your case, take it to the judge, through your attorney.

The bureaucracy of DFCS makes it difficult sometimes to create change or improvement. Your attorney can consult with the attorney for DFCS to prompt movement. Or your attorney can move for a hearing to air out the issues. You have a limited time to accomplish the goals of the Case Plan. Pointing at DFCS later won't get back the time wasted, so act when the issues arise rather than trying to take action later.

Right To Change Mind about Services – But Don't Wait Too Long

In some cases, a parent, due to outside circumstances, might decide to have a non-reunification case plan. A non-reunification case plan means that the parent receives no services, no visits, and generally no chance of getting the child back.

A parent can change their mind and ask for a different case plan. This change might require some action by the parent to establish trust with DFCS before reestablishing contact with the child.

Right To Be Involved in Education Decisions and Receive Information Relating to School

A parent's right to be involved in a child's life includes being given notice about and participating in decisions relating to education. Asserting the right to be involved with your child's education may be challenging in that transportation may be unavailable and scheduling may be beyond your control, but you can be involved. Discuss the issues, concerns, and praises relating to your child's education with the school, DFCS, and foster parents, if that's permitted. Staying involved for your child not only shows your ongoing interest; it also maintains that relationship with your child.

Right To Attend School Functions and Extracurricular Functions

In most cases, the goal of the Case Plan is to reunify parent and child. Maintaining that bond with your child includes supporting your child at school and attending extracurricular functions. Creating a contact with DFCS and/or the foster parents in order to obtain this information is key to remaining in touch for these matters. The Court can order this if asked, but working with the group to support your child creates healthier relationships.

Right To Be Involved in Decisions concerning Religious Instruction

Religion can be a difficult subject to tackle. A parent might be able to influence religious instruction if strict religious practices have been kept up to the time of foster care. Proclaimed religious practices which endanger a child's health, safety, and well-being would certainly be subject to the Court's review and may require modification to provide for the health of the child.

Right To Be Heard on Name of Child in Foster Care

On occasion, foster parents may choose to call a child by that child's middle name rather than the name used by the biological parents. This issue can be raised with the Court. In most cases, the decision will be to defer to the parents' preference for the child's name.

Section Two

Working the Case Plan

Chapter 1

Learn the System.

One day, you are fighting in court to bring your child back. The next day the Court decides that you must work a case plan before your child can come home. This dramatic shift requires modifying your view of Child Protective Services (CPS). Changing how you see CPS so that you can get your children back is a difficult transition. The earlier fighting can create a lot of anger and quite a bit of hurt on the part of a parent, but for the sake of your goal—which is getting your children back—you must make the effort and make this change.

After the Court orders parents to complete a case plan and decides that children cannot go home yet, many people want to continue to fight with CPS, the judge, and anyone associated with CPS about the issues that were addressed in court. That feeling is completely understandable. You may think, "How can a parent work with people who said the things to the judge that were said about that parent?"

Here's the challenge: The rules change once the Court makes those decisions. These rules differ from the rules in social life. Sometimes a parent may be tempted to fight with CPS by "winning" small battles: being late for meetings, not returning phone calls, claiming to be sick, being mean when it's not necessary.

Inconveniencing the people at CPS or people who do the work for CPS may provide you some immediate satisfaction. In the long run, though, these small moments that feel like winning create a pattern of negative behavior that **will** be communicated to the Court. These small things parents do to feel better in the short term pile up and actually make the parents look bad in front of the judge. When three or four people report to the judge these same types of behavior, the judge will take notice and hold your actions against you.

What can a parent do when everything tells them to fight back?

Learn To Navigate the System.

Learn to follow the rules to bring a beloved child home and get away from CPS/Court.

These rules for dealing with CPS <u>can</u> be learned. If you can apply these new rules, CPS and service providers will have positive reports about your behavior. You <u>can</u> bring your child home. To change behavior requires constant practice, but if you can learn and apply these rules, you <u>can</u> be successful.

Dealing with CPS requires a long-term strategy. Accomplishing the goal of getting your child home will take time. You must focus on the ultimate outcome. No one questions that a parent will want to feel better and empowered in the face of government employees who may have made your life so unpleasant, but do not lose sight of your goals. The plan to regain custody of your child must focus on the long term. Remember that each encounter with CPS or a service provider produces a report. Understanding that good, positive reports will bring your child home is the most important first step.

Parents, in most cases, have a right to a reunification case plan. This plan creates the roadmap to children returning home. The change in attitude helps bring children home faster.

Learn the Social Rules of Interaction To Get Better Reports to the Court.

Chapter 2

Succeed with Truth.

"How do I fight liars? How? How do I get my children back? They have all the power and resources and the judge is on their side."

To regain custody of your child and get Child Protective Services out of your life, you need to change strategy. Continuing to resist CPS and refusing to work on the case plan/safety plan only hurts you **and** your child.

CPS workers are not injured, harmed, or hurt by your failure to start and finish the goals of your case plan. Their job requires note-taking and reports on your behavior as well as their efforts toward helping you complete your case plan, so that they can testify to the Court later.

The harder you resist CPS, the less likely you are to get your child back. Is that really what you want? Is your pride so important to you that you would give up your child just to prove CPS wrong?

Are you prepared to lose your right to your child because you hate CPS? Failing to work the case plan makes it harder and harder for you to get your child back. The law, whether we like it or not, requires that you make substantial progress on your case plan. If you don't complete the case plan as quickly as possible, you will lose valuable time with your child. Georgia law declares a child abandoned if the parent fails to visit a child for six months. After 12 to 15 months, if you, the parent, have not made progress on your case plan, Child Protective Services will have to consider asking the Court to terminate your rights to your child.

With the changes I discuss in this book, you can take charge and take control of how the case progresses. If you fail to complete your case, that is YOUR choice. Take responsibility for being present for appointments. You may feel powerless, but in fact <u>you</u> are in control. <u>You</u> make decisions about what <u>you</u> will do. CPS does not control <u>how you react</u> and the choices you make. Prove to the Court that you've changed.

Take Charge. Act on Your Case Plan.

Chapter 3

Trust Issues.

"How do I trust the people who took my child?"

Here's what's important here: **you don't have to trust them in order to do your part of the case plan**. You can either work on the case plan and follow this advice, or you can just give up. Accepting the referrals CPS makes and working with these rules is the only way to ensure that you make progress on your case plan. While it is acceptable for a parent to find independent services and pay for those, the fees and timetables for private, independent services vary.

Losing custody of your child to CPS is very hard to accept. But once a court has given CPS custody, you must move on from the hurt and anger of losing custody, no matter how bad you feel about your situation. Do not expect anyone else to know or understand how you feel. What is important right now is for you to realize that the time for you to complete your case plan began running the day your child entered CPS care.

You must start **working toward and** achieving the goals on your case plan. If you do not make significant progress on your case plan in 13 months—that is, one year and one month— CPS must begin to look for other, permanent placements, like adoptive homes, for your child.

As a parent who loves your child, you must find a way to focus on the steps of your case plan. The steps in this book may be new for you or just a reminder of advice you have heard from others, but having them here, in writing, **in one place**, will help you stick to them. These rules will help you in your struggle with CPS and service providers. Following this advice will empower you to complete your case plan.

Focus on the Case Plan.
Don't Focus on the People at CPS.

Chapter 4

One Step at a Time.

"I don't have time for all of this."

Having a full ~~is~~ life is certainly a challenge. You choose what is most important. Do you want your child in your house? In your life? Then you will change your priorities and your thoughts about what is important.

Know the steps of your case plan. Look at that document. Understand what the judge has ordered you to do. Ask your lawyer for help if you do not understand your case plan.

Break the case plan goals into smaller steps. No one expects you to do everything at one time. Figure out what you have to do first, then next, then next to accomplish the goal; and write down on the back of your case plan, or perhaps in a notebook, a list of the smaller steps necessary to complete your case plan. Check off each smaller step as you complete it. Marking items off will help you see the progress that you are making.

Make your child and your case plan your priorities, the most important things in your life. Completing the steps on your case plan should be your PRIORITY while your child is in CPS custody. Finishing the case plan quickly shows that your child is more important than anything else.

Be careful about the advice you follow. Many times our friends and family tell us what <u>they</u> think should be important. They may try to influence the choices we make or cause us to spend too much time focusing on the past. Hanging around with family and friends who are not aiding you with your case plan and supporting you toward accomplishing those steps is not helpful.

Instead, spend time with family and friends who encourage your efforts to complete your case plans. Cooperative family and friends create an important support system for completing a case plan when they are helping you achieve goals.

You, and only you, can complete the steps on your case plan. Finishing steps on your case plan will show the Judge, the

Guardian *ad litem*, and CPS that you care and you want your child back with you.

You have a right to a copy of your case plan. You should receive a copy of the Case Plan for the child. If you do not, request a copy from CPS.

Also, for goals that are unfamiliar to you, find out how many steps may be involved. Making a doctor's appointment is routine. Setting up a psychological evaluation may require more steps.

Remember to notify CPS of appointments as well

Track Your Case Plan

Chapter 5

Priorities.

"I'm too busy for visits and case plans."

Visits with your child are the most important step in your case plan. Maintaining a bond and relationship with your child is critical. If you fail to visit your child for six months, the Court can consider that to be abandonment and grounds to terminate your parental rights. The requirements of the case plan and timing of your visits might not be scheduled at the best times for you, but you **must** make these things work.

Buy a calendar or use an internet-based calendar that can be accessed by your phone. Inputting the appointments and keeping track of them will aid you in knowing ahead of time what might complicate your schedule for seeing your child and help you eliminate those complications ahead of time. Check that calendar periodically so that appointments don't sneak up on you.

Many appointments may be scheduled at inconvenient times. You told the judge you would do whatever it takes to get your child home. Prove it.

No excuses. When you make your child your priority and choose to put your feet on the path to completing your case plan, you show that you understand that planning to do the things required of you is most important. "I couldn't get a ride," "I forgot," "I had to work," "I didn't have money to put minutes on my phone"... these are not good reasons for missing out on a necessary step of your case plan. Every meeting is important. Every therapy session is a priority.

You are in charge of your schedule. If you truly cannot attend a meeting or a session, call the person ahead of time and reschedule. "Ahead of time" means as long beforehand as you can. Calling on the morning of the meeting or, worse, an hour before the meeting is not good enough unless you are in the emergency room and can provide a medical excuse that shows you had a life-threatening medical problem.

Judges want to know that you are responsible. A responsible parent plans ahead. If you have a job that makes scheduling more difficult, discuss this situation with service providers and CPS and your lawyer. Employment and income are important parts of the overall goals. Find a way to work out these conflicts well in advance of meetings.

Ignoring the problems will not make them go away. Denying the conflicts or that problems exist will make them worse. Take charge of your case plan by planning ahead. Show the Court you are being a responsible parent by managing your schedule and being on time for appointments.

Visit Your Child. Maintain that Bond.

Chapter 6

Different Expectations.

"Why am I punished for being 15 minutes late?"

Life presents us with a variety of situations. These situations have different social rules. It's okay to be late by 15 minutes in personal situations. But you would not intentionally be late for court, would you? These appointments are court-ordered. Make sure you're on time for appointments just like you would be for court.

Use the alarm function on your cell phone to remind you. Be sure to set the alarm to provide enough time to travel to the appointment.

Be on time. Arriving at the scheduled time, or even slightly early, shows that you respect the time of the people with whom you are meeting as well as the importance of the scheduled appointment. Being timely also tells the people with whom you are meeting that you are responsible. Most importantly, in this dependency case, being on time tells CPS that you are making your child your one and only priority.

CPS will report missed visits and late arrivals to the judge. If you're on time, there is nothing negative to report.

Be On Time. Create Alarms to Remind Yourself.

Chapter 7

Calendar Control.

"There are too many requirements in this case plan."

The case plan may place many time-consuming appointments on your already busy calendar. Being busy sometimes causes stress, even for people who do not have to deal with Child Protective Services. You would probably benefit from sitting down and making a schedule. You <u>can</u> control your schedule and what you are expected to do. BUT it requires planning on your part.

As a parent, you are expected to keep appointments, make sure your child is on time for school and school events, ensure that your child is ready when the school bus arrives, care for your child's health, and deal with many other responsibilities.

Parents oftentimes sacrifice their personal priorities to create time for their children's needs. Evaluate your schedule. Look at each item on that schedule. What is more important, getting your child back or doing that other item on your schedule?

Sit down one day each week to look at your schedule. What events are on your calendar? Do you have time to hang out with your friends? Planning ahead helps you keep your goals in mind as you think about your time.

During the time your child is in CPS care, you need to be on time and prepared for appointments. These appointments are with people who will make recommendations about when your child will come home. Missed appointments suggest that you do not understand the importance of responsibility and time management. If you frequently miss appointments or show up late, those individuals will tell the Court. You give up your control when you let others make negative reports because you failed to plan.

Learning and applying time management skills will help you in other areas of life as well as with your case plan. One of the requirements for you is to maintain employment and stable housing. Finding and keeping a job also requires time management skills.

Taking control of your schedule means taking control of your progress on your case plan. The more good and positive reports to the Court, the more progress you will make on your case plan.

Create a Calendar and Keep a Schedule.

Chapter 8

Be the Bigger Person.

"CPS treats me like I'm not a person."

After fighting CPS in court and dealing with case managers, you feel like they don't show you any respect and disregard your requests and needs. Like it or not, believe it or not, if you treat them better than they treat you, they will change their tune. You cannot control their behavior, but you can control how you treat them, and everyone else.

CPS is not your family or your friends. Don't expect them to forgive and forget how you may have treated them during the process. You may feel that CPS and the Court are asking you to do a lot and not asking nicely. These CPS and Court requirements are standard in most cases. This process has many important steps. Remember that the CPS case manager and therapists and anyone else CPS sends will be making recommendations to the Court.

Be polite and courteous. If you disagree with CPS, do so politely. Disagreement does not mean that someone has to raise their voice or be insulting.

Spend time considering how you will respond to CPS workers and service providers. What, if anything, can you do to change your response to the negative interactions? Remember: you are responsible for how you respond. Thinking ahead about the best way to respond will prepare you for the real-life interactions. Giving thought to strategies will help you prepare for the return of your child and their potential misbehavior.

Being polite also does not mean that you must like CPS, or anyone else. Courtesy shows that you put aside how you feel about the individuals involved in the case and that you will do what needs to be done so your child can come home.

When your child is in CPS custody, you have little to no control over many things. This lack of control and lack of knowledge about your child's day-to-day well-being naturally creates frustration and concern about your child. That frustration should not be taken out on CPS or others sent to assist you with your case plan. Take the energy of that frustration and use it to fuel your positive progress to complete your case plan as soon as possible. Making the goals of the case plan your priority shows CPS your <u>child</u> is your priority.

You may find that CPS workers become upset when you "get in their faces." In personal conflict, some people use direct confrontation, or getting in the other person's face, as a way to resolve disputes. This strategy may work in social situations, but in formal circumstances, this behavior could be taken as threatening and lead to criminal charges.

The best practice is to avoid "getting in the face of" service providers, CPS, and Court personnel. Strategies for calm behavior include taking a moment to breathe before speaking or simply excusing yourself and walking away for a moment.

When addressing conflict in this formal setting, using a calm voice will work better and be more effective than using a raised voice. Service providers, CPS, and the Court are not your social friends and will not be forgiving of "getting in their face."

You might also speak with your therapist or parent aide about strategies for addressing this frustration.

You control how you treat other people. If you are polite, they can only report that you are polite. Taking frustration out on others will create the impression that you are not interested in completing your case plan and not interested in the return of your child. THE CHOICE IS YOURS. Being frustrated and angry leads to poor choices. Poor choices lead to major problems and mistakes that could make it more difficult for you to have your child returned.

Choose to be polite.
Choose Your Child Over Your Anger.

Chapter 9

What's Important.

"I can't keep minutes on my phone and I miss calls and messages. Then they say I've messed up."

Minutes for your phone are expensive. Think about how you use your phone. What's more important, having minutes available to talk to people about getting your child back, or talking to your friends?

One responsibility you have is to be available by phone. If that means having a phone that you only use for CPS related issues and nothing or no one else, then you should do it. In most cases, CPS and service providers will contact you by phone. If your phone has no minutes, or if you change phones and phone numbers frequently without notifying CPS, your attorney, and/or service providers, you will miss important information and important contacts.

Track the minutes remaining on your phone. If minutes are low, use texting to communicate with friends and family. Reserve the minutes for communicating with service providers and CPS.

Think of it this way: if your child had an emergency, you would want to know. Having minutes on your phone means being available for your child.

Missing those contacts means that you fail to get critical information about appointments and your child's well-being. When you miss this information, you fail to meet your case plan goals. You can stay on track with your case plan by setting priorities for phone usage.

Use Your Phone Only for Important Business When Your Minutes are Low.

Chapter 10

Show Commitment.

"They act like I don't care for MY child."

If you show up for all your appointments, keep visits with your child, and treat people with respect, no one will be able to say that. If you fail to act responsibly in appearing for appointments and spending time with your child, then what else should they think?

Your <u>actions</u> show everyone your commitment. Show them you are responsible. Being on time, keeping a phone, establishing a stable home and stable employment, keeping appointments, and being prepared show the Court that you take the case plan seriously. Your actions speak much louder than anyone's words.

When a child is in their home, parents are required to provide shelter, provide education, provide medical treatment, and to feed, clothe, love, and comfort their children. Your ability to maintain consistency and stability will overcome the attitudes of those involved in the case.

When your child is in CPS care, show the Court that you understand that the things the Court asks you to do are just as important. Until you show you are able to care for your child responsibly, the Court will not let your child go home with you. You are responsible for proving these things. No one else will do it for you.

How can you show this responsibility while your child is in care? Visit with your child. Show the bond you have with your child. Keep appointments. Complete your case plan. Make sure you have minutes on your phone so that you can be contacted. Give CPS only good things to report about your behavior and progress on your case plan.

Show You Care by Keeping Appointments and Returning Phone Calls.

Chapter 11

Choices.

"CPS can't decide whom I see."

You are absolutely right. You choose to see whomever you want.

Understand, though, that if the person you want to see, including a spouse or significant other, is charged with hurting you, your child, or someone else's child, no court in the world will choose your side. The Court will always choose to protect the child.

Decide whether people in your life are helping or hurting your efforts to bring your child home. Look at their actions, not what they tell you. If a person is not helping you complete your case plan, distance yourself.

You must choose your child and choose to protect your child. As you work your case plan, you may find that your partner (husband, wife, boyfriend, girlfriend) is holding you back.

If you see that you must choose between your partner and your child, choose your child. Your partner is an adult and should be able to care for himself/herself. Your child did not choose you or your partner as parents. A child is a lifetime commitment. Choose your child. If you do not choose your child, choosing your partner may cause you to lose your child.

If you choose an adult over your child, understand that the Court will choose your child and hold your choice against you. Once the Court becomes involved, the Court's job is the best interest of the child. Not you.

If you are involved in a violent or abusive relationship, use CPS to help you find advice and aid you to get out of that relationship. At least ask for advice somewhere. Find the best way to leave.

In some cases, a parent must choose between their significant other and their child. Ignoring this choice is just like choosing the partner. Choose your child by completing your case plan and avoiding those people the Court says to avoid.

**Choose Your Child Over
Any Other Person in Your Life.**

Chapter 12

When CPS Errs.

"CPS hasn't done their job."

CPS may not have done everything. You may be right.

CPS is not perfect. None of this advice suggests that CPS cannot be challenged. A mistake by CPS, however, is not necessarily a defense that will get your child home more quickly.

Your failure to meet goals will not be excused because CPS made a mistake. If CPS fails to meet their obligations, it might make CPS look bad, but it will not change what you did or did not do.

If you are scheduled for a hearing, ask to be represented by an attorney. The <u>attorney</u> can point out the problems with CPS's work. But remember, CPS's failure does not make you less responsible for the case plan.

When CPS fails to do their job utterly and completely, the judge will give you more time to accomplish goals. The failure of CPS does not return your child.

Failures by CPS
Do Not Automatically Mean a Win for You.

Chapter 13

Keep Asking.

"I need to change the case plan. No one listens."

The Court changes case plans. If you would like to change something about your case plan, ask very clearly. Just complaining about an issue will not qualify as a request for a change. Ask for changes <u>through your attorney</u> when CPS doesn't listen.

Change happens when you ask very clearly and specifically for the change you want. Sometimes people **believe** complaining about the same problem constantly will lead to a resolution. In CPS cases, you should be direct about the changes you wish to see happen.

If you do not work well with a service provider, ask politely for a different provider. Be able to say **clearly** and **exactly** why you would like to change.

Parents tend to stop working with a provider when things are uncomfortable for them. **But** if you simply stop working on a case plan step, the Court will consider this choice a failure to meet a goal of the case plan. Asking for a different provider and stating the reason is the responsible way to handle the matter. The Court will be more willing to help with that change if you ask directly.

Even if you do all this, you may be asked to continue working with that provider. Do the best that you can. Normally, you should continue to do the best you can with the provider you have.

Speak with Your Lawyer About Your Concerns.
Make Sure the Problem is Clear to CPS and the Judge.

Chapter 14

Make the Most of Time.

"How do I prove I can parent in only one hour a week? I don't see my child enough."

That is a valid point. Choose to be involved in your child's life.

For more time with your child, ask to be included in doctor's appointments, therapy progress, school events, church or community events in which your child is involved. Ask to attend these events when you can. Be supportive. Show everyone that you can accomplish the case plan, but also do more. Ask to be able to speak with your child's teachers. Find out what you can do to support the child's needs during visits. Be a proactive parent.

If you tell your child or someone else that you will attend an event, a doctor's appointment, a school meeting, **be there**. Don't make promises you can't keep. Those kinds of promises will make you look less responsible.

When you show up, put down your phone. Whatever is happening in that room with your child, or in your meeting about your child, is more important than anything on your phone. Participate. Be present and attentive.

During your visitation, you should make the most of that time.

To be in control when it comes to visits, (1) be on time and (2) be ready. Spend time with your child. Let go of any concerns you have with CPS or visit supervisors. During visits: read a book with your child, ask about school, ask about what the child did that day, be the parent. Have fun. Use the lessons you've learned from parenting classes or instruction. When behavior needs to be redirected, do that. If you need help, ask for it.

How do you maintain control in this situation? Control your behavior. Visit supervisors will report to the Court about how visits progress. If you followed the advice and suggestions from your sessions, the supervisor will only have good things to say.

You are the Parent. Do Not Forget That.

Focus on Your Child.

Use Every Minute You can Find to Spend Quality Time with Your Child.

Chapter 15

Record Keeping.

"I call and call. No one calls me back."

Keep track of all calls and every other contact with CPS and other providers. Keep a notebook. This notebook will give you control. Know when you called and why you called because you made a habit of keeping track. **Write it down every time.** A simple spiral-bound notebook will work for this purpose.

- Write down the dates and times that you spoke with CPS or met with providers and each time you attempt to call CPS or service providers.

- Write down who you spoke to about your case/your child.

- If you are given instructions by these people, write them down. Repeat the instructions to the person giving the instructions so that you and the person giving instructions agree about what was asked of you.

- Keep track of the places you make application for jobs.

- Make a note of the homework you have from providers.

- Note the phone numbers and names of people you speak with so that you do not lose those important pieces of information.

- Collect receipts for items you purchase for your child.

-Keep track of any money spent on your child and the dates and amounts of any child support payments. You can staple or tape these onto a page of the notebook, or you can put them in a plastic bag.

If you have a court date, you can use this notebook to remind yourself about the people with whom you have contact and the dates you spoke with them. This notebook can be very helpful for your lawyer as well. You may find that you have better notes than CPS. Use the contact log on page 98.

Keep Track of Your Contacts to Support Your Efforts.

Chapter 16

Monetary Support.

"They expect me to pay child support."

Yes. You are required to pay child support. Your child is entitled to child support. It's the law in most states.

Understand that if the child were in your home, you would be required to support your child. Even if the child is not in your home, the law says that you still are responsible for supporting your child.

Even if you are unable to supply the full amount, pay something. Participate in the process of child support court and determining your payment amount. Document the percentage of your income that you are paying, even if it is only a small portion.

Do not get upset when you are asked to provide support. You are the parent and you are responsible, like it or not. If you can't pay child support, the Court might take that as evidence that you would be unable to feed, clothe, and provide stable housing for your child if your child was in your home.

Complaining about child support will not help you get your child home. If you aren't paying child support but spend money on your hair, nails, and fancy clothes, the Court will notice. The Court knows how much those things cost. Everyone will know and they will call you on it.

Point out to CPS what government benefits would be available if your child were in your custody. If you are able to support yourself, you should make every effort to show that you are supporting yourself.

Do What You Can to Support Your Child Financially by Paying the Child Support.

Chapter 17

Employment.

"Jobs don't just drop out of thin air."

Having and keeping a job is usually a goal of a case plan. Generally, parents must be employed in order to support a household—pay rent and utilities, buy food, clothing, and provide for transportation.

If you're having trouble finding a job, keep looking. Maintain a record of each job for which you apply, and with whom you speak. Use a notebook as discussed in the previous chapter. Be sure to have minutes on your phone.

No job is beneath you. Do whatever it takes to obtain legal, legitimate employment.

If you have a job, be sure to keep documentation of how much you receive each pay period. CPS will need to see proof of your employment.

Financially Supporting Your Child is Part of Parenting.

Chapter 18

Family Tree.

"Why do they want to know about my family when I'm getting my child back?"

Hard to believe, but your family and close friends—that is, fictive kin—may be a better resource than foster parents. Always provide CPS with a list of family members who can care for your child instead of some stranger. CPS is required to contact your family, with or without your help. Your cooperation shows the Court your willingness to work the program. Family is a great resource for you, and placing your child with family makes better family connections for you.

Make a list of all the living relatives you can think of and where they live. If you have close friends who are reliable and consistent in your child's life, add them for consideration, too. These family and fictive kin can divert your child from foster care--government custody--which provides more time for you to obtain services without the pressure of a looming termination.

Also, foster families can be hours away. If you have trouble with transportation, you might not be able to see your child as often as you could because you can't get to the foster home, and CPS won't always provide transportation. Placing your child with family closer to you would make visits easier.

In 2020, Georgia law changed slightly as relates to placement. If a family member who was duly notified of the need for placement fails to take advantage of the right within six (6) months of the notice, then DFCS/CPS is excused from considering that family member.

Also, if a child is in a stable home of a caregiver for 12 months and a court finds that removal of the child from that placement is against the best interest of the child, then DFCS/CPS would not be compliant with the law if DFCS/CPS moves the child.

The old preference for family, fictive kin, and parents is slowly going away. A parent's preference over all other caregivers is no longer the priority. Following the case plan faster is more important than ever.

Cooperate with CPS to Find Potential Family Placements.

Chapter 19

Attitude.

Over the time you have an open CPS case, you will encounter people who mean well and want to help. These people, in all likelihood, grew up in different circumstances than you did. These folks may not understand the challenges that you have faced. Some of these people will be part of a citizen's review panel for DFCS cases.

Yet, these well-meaning people will report negatively about you when you have a bad day or make a negative comment. Engaging with people politely may create a difference in how these folks receive you and how they treat you. You do not have to be best friends with these folks but you should if at all possible be polite and help them understand your situation.

In some cases, these people from different backgrounds, when given the opportunity to understand your situation can become your biggest advocates with CPS and the court.

Being Polite to those who Do Not Understand Does Not Cost Anything.

Being Rude Will Impact How People See You.

Chapter 20

Tests.

"How many tests before I get my child back?"

Could be one, could be several. These tests are very important. Cooperating with testers and in taking these tests will impact what is reported to the court. You control how these individuals talk about you. Remember that. You may be asked to complete written or verbal tests with a psychologist or social worker.

- Be on time. Do not miss appointments. (Make sure that your phone is working. They will call you.)

- Answer the questions honestly. These tests are written in such a way that the person giving the test can figure out if you're trying to lie to make yourself sound better. **A statement that you were dishonest on the test will be included in the written evaluation if the tester finds that you were not being honest. A report about lying does not make things easier for you.**

- Just because you don't think you have the problem which the test is about does not mean that you should avoid or ignore the test. These types of tests might include assessments for anger, drugs, alcohol, domestic violence, child abuse, trauma assessment, or any other issues. Failure to complete the test is failure to meet a case plan goal.

- You should have a second meeting with the psychologist/social worker who does any psychological or other evaluations. At that time the psychologist/social worker will review the evaluator's recommendations. These recommendations are important. Ask the psychologist any questions you might have.

- You will probably be required to follow these recommendations. Be sure that you understand them clearly.

These tests and meetings are goals in your case plan.

You should keep track of the goals of your case plan in your notebook as discussed in Chapter 15. You might also keep track of what provider is serving as therapist, psychologist, or CASA, and even who your case manager is by writing it in your notebook. Select a page in your notebook for keeping track of contacts/providers.

Treat Medical and Psychological Tests like any other Court-ordered Step.

Chapter 21

Paternity is NOT Magic.

"DNA says I'm the father. Give me my child."

If you have just discovered that you are a father from a DNA test, do not expect that the Court will immediately hand you the child and send you home together. As a putative father, you will need to establish a relationship with this child and prove that you can meet the child's needs before your child can come home with you. You must show the Court that your home is the best place for and in the best interest of the child.

But first, a putative father must legitimate to become a party to a case. Legitimation during a DFCS/CPS case is easier and less costly than going through Superior Court. A court must find that the putative father is both the legal parent and that it is in the child's best interest that the paternity be declared.

Build a bond with your child. Take any tests and classes offered very seriously.

If you have an established relationship with this child, you might be in a better position to take your child home. Establishing a history of financial and emotional support will make a case for your existing relationship with your child. The Court will not send a child home with a stranger. DNA does not create an automatic bond or relationship with a child. Creating a bond with a child takes time and effort on the parent's part.

Take any parenting classes seriously. Show that you want to be a parent. Visit with the child as often as you are permitted. Establishing a relationship and bond with your child is critical.

In either case, be sure to provide a list of family members who might be good options for placement until you complete your case plan. Family members who have raised children will be particularly good options. Family members can also provide positive support for you while you continue to make progress.

Being a Parent is More Than DNA.
Focus on Building a Relationship.

Chapter 22

Cast of Characters.

"Who are all these people anyway?"

Having trouble keeping up with all these people with jobs of which you've never heard? Here's a list of some.

Judge: Attorney, appointed or elected, who makes decisions in a case based on the law and the facts presented in Court. Enforces case plans, determines whether children go home.

Parents' Attorney (or your attorney): either appointed to you or hired by you, this is a lawyer to represent your interests, provide you the best advice given your circumstances, and advocate for you in court. Make sure you tell this lawyer everything about your case.

State's Attorney: The attorney who represents CPS. This person looks out for CPS's interests, not yours.

Guardian ad litem (GAL): Attorney designated by the Judge to look out for the child's best interests and make recommendations to the Court. These recommendations do not have to be what your child wants, only what that attorney believes is in the best interests of the child. This person might observe your visits with your child.

Child's Attorney: Your child will be appointed an attorney to represent the child's interests. This attorney will tell the Court what your child wants and does not take direction from you. This attorney has a different goal from the GAL.

Court Appointed Special Advocate (CASA): Community volunteers who work with children to advocate for the child's best interest. These unpaid individuals work to bond with children and give them a voice on a more daily basis to supplement the GAL's work in court. This person might observe your visits with your child. CASAs do not work for CPS. They are independent.

CPS Case Manager: Person employed by CPS to make referrals for you and your child, to track down putative fathers, to make monthly contact with you and your child. This person makes reports to the Court about compliance with the case plan, visits, and contacts with you. The Case Manager has several listings because case managers change with regularity.

CPS Supervisor: The person supervising your case manager. If you can't find your case manager, the supervisor is the person to call.

Psychologist: A doctor with a Ph.D. or Psy.D. who may give written and verbal tests to you and your child. A psychologist may also provide therapy for you and/or your child. Someone hired by CPS as an outside contractor who provides service for a fee.

Social worker: Someone hired by CPS as an outside contractor, someone who doesn't work at CPS, who provides service for a fee. A social worker may give tests. A social worker can provide therapy for you.

Parent aide: A person who may supervise visits with your child, and who may provide transportation for you and/or your child to visits. This person might also provide parenting instruction. This person is someone who doesn't work at CPS.

Visitation supervisor: A person trained to observe your visit, make notes about the visit, intervene if behaviors are not appropriate, and report to the CPS and the Court about visits.

Know who you are speaking with and what their role is.

Chapter 23

Always Ask for A Lawyer.

It bears repeating: **Always, always, always request an attorney.** You should request an attorney to help navigate the Court processes. Attorneys understand the Court rules and the requirements that CPS must follow.

The attorney cannot complete the case plan for you. If a crisis arises, however, the attorney can help you ask the judge for changes. Keep your attorney up to date on what is happening in your case. Given time to prepare, an attorney can advocate around issues that are important to you and find witnesses when appropriate.

Always Request an Attorney.

Chapter 24

Disagreement with Diagnosis.

"That doctor is wrong. There's nothing wrong with me."

If you disagree with the doctor, ask to get a second opinion. However, perhaps talking to an independent person about the stresses in your life, like your child's being in State custody, might help you.

Please understand, a doctor may diagnose a mental health concern or a medical concern. Always ask the doctor questions. Remember that you can ask for a second opinion about your diagnosis from another doctor. Work with providers to find alternatives. Consider the medical advice. Consider the medication. Above all, do not stop the treatment. Do not ignore the diagnosis. Work on the treatment and continue to talk with providers. Consider and discuss your concerns.

Ignoring the diagnosis is NOT the way to succeed in your case plan. Actively working on resolving a medical issue or disagreement will be more impressive to the court than ignoring it or arguing with a doctor.

If CPS is not listening, contact your attorney. Your lawyer can bring the issue to the Court for discussion and perhaps convince the Court to change your case plan.

Challenging the Doctors Must be Done through the Court.

Chapter 25

Drug Testing.

"I don't have a drug problem."

The Court may require substance abuse testing. These tests could include verbal and written tests, but may also require drug screens. You may believe that "recreational" drug use is a personal choice. The Court will make drugs screens a requirement of your case plan.

Following the recommendations of the evaluator will be a part of the Court's order. These steps, even if you disagree with them, are required in order for you to bring your child home.

The Court will be concerned about any illegal drug use. While marijuana is legal in some states, the drug remains illegal in most states. In addition, use of marijuana requires an investment of money in something that does not further your efforts to bring your child home. If you can afford illegal drugs, you can pay child support.

The law requires clean drug screens for a specific period of time if children have been removed due to substance abuse. Remember CPS has timelines, in which to start Termination proceedings.

Drug Evaluations are Common.
Cooperation with the Tests Gets You Through the
Case Plan More Quickly.

Chapter 26

Fair Game.

"My social media is not evidence."

Yes, it can be, actually. What you post on social media, on Facebook, Twitter, or any other internet platform that is open to the public is fair game, even if the judge never hears about it. The CPS workers will tell the judge what you said to them that was not in your best interest and contrary to your case plan. Your social media, if printed out and verified to have come from your account, is you telling a judge what you have done since the last court appearance.

The best idea is to <u>avoid social media altogether</u>. If you believe that staying on social media is something you must do, then be cautious. Please understand that what you say on the internet stays on the internet—it can always be recovered even if you've deleted it.

Returning to a relationship that the Court has deemed inappropriate for your children and talking about that on social media can come back to hurt you in your efforts to regain your children.

Openly writing or posting photos about use of drugs or alcohol can also be damaging to case.

Be smart. Do not talk about your case or your personal problems or flaunt your social activities where CPS case managers can find your words.

Avoiding Social media Altogether is the Best Choice.

If You Must Use It, though, Post Good and Positive Events in Your Life.

Chapter 27

Requirements.

"What happens if I don't finish all this stuff?"

Like it or not, you have a case plan to start <u>and</u> finish. You control how you respond and whether you finish your case plan. You make choices every day that say something about whether you want your child home. These choices do not always seem as if they impact your custody, but they do.

Make choices each day that focus on bringing your child home.

In many cases, CPS must make a referral to a service provider so that you can accomplish specific goals on your case plan. If CPS has failed to make the referral and provide you with a service to accomplish a particular step in your case plan, you should communicate that to your attorney. Before any hearing, the lawyer needs to prepare ahead of time to raise these issues.

Failure to make progress and work your case plan means failure, period. Your case plan is a road map for the return of your child. If you fail to keep appointments and to make progress on your case plan, your child will stay in CPS custody longer. The longer your child is in CPS custody, the more likely it is that you will be subject to a trial for termination of your parental rights.

You do not have to like CPS. But once your child is in CPS custody, you need to find a way to work with CPS and the other providers assigned to work with you. If you FAIL to accomplish your goals, that failure lies at your feet. Keeping in contact with CPS is important.

Stopping work on a step of the case plan because you do not like something about the step means that you **failed** to accomplish the step. Failing to complete the case plan means that your child will stay with CPS. Period.

**You Must Substantially Complete Your Case Plan.
No One Can Do That But You.**

Chapter 28

Source of Change.

If you make substantial progress on your case plan, the Court will consider sending your child home. Keeping a stable home, finding steady employment, checking off those tasks on your case plan mean that you will find that the judge is happy to see you.

This change is not from anything anyone else did. The change happened in you. By following the guidance in this book, you will change your situation on your own.

Remembering these guidelines, you will improve your chances of success in other parts of your life.

Completing Your Case Plan Goals Brings You Stability and Will Place You in a Position to Bring Your Child Home.

Case Plan Conclusion

By taking control of your choices and treating people politely and with respect, you will gain respect more quickly. Following these simple steps will place you on your way toward successfully completing your case plan. You can follow these easy instructions and accomplish your goals.

Quick Reference Reminder

Learn the social rules of interaction to get better reports to the Court.

Take charge. Act on your case plan.

Focus on the case plan. Don't focus on the people at CPS.

Know the case plan goals. Break each goal into smaller steps. You will see progress.

Visit your child. Maintain that bond.

Be on time. Create alarms to remind yourself.

Create a calendar and keep a schedule.

Choose to be polite. Choose your child over your anger.

Use your phone only for important business when your minutes are low

Show you care by keeping appointments and returning phone calls.

Choose your child over any other person in your life.

Failures by CPS do not automatically mean a win for you.

Speak with your lawyer about your concerns. Make sure the problem is clear to CPS and the judge.

You are the parent. Do not forget that. Focus on your child. Use every minute you find to spend quality time with your child.

Keep track of your contacts to support your efforts.

Do what you can to support your child financially by paying child support.

Financially supporting your child is part of parenting.

Being polite to those who do not understand does not cost anything.

Being rude will impact how people see you.

Treat medical and psychological tests like any other court-ordered step.

Being a parent is more than DNA. Focus on building a relationship.

Know whom you are speaking with and what their role is.

Always request an attorney

Cooperate with CPS to find potential family placements.

Challenging the doctors must be done through the court.

Drug evaluations are common.

Cooperation with the tests gets you through the case plan more quickly.

Avoiding social media altogether is the best choice. If you must use it, though, post good and positive events in your life.

You must substantially complete your case plan. No one can do that but you.

Completing your case plan goals brings you stability and will place you in a position to bring your child home.

Section Three

Words, Phrases, & Definitions

This glossary serves as a guide for the terms used in the book as well as in DFCS cases. The definitions are exactly the same and placed at the back of the book for ease of location.

Care Coordinator: The State licenses private agencies to provide many of the mental health and family services mentioned in this book. Each private agency will assign a person to locate appropriate services and make contact with clients maintain consistent treatment.

CASA-Court Appointed Special Advocate: Community volunteers who work with children to advocate for the child's best interest. These unpaid individuals work to bond with children and give them a voice on a more daily basis to supplement the GAL's work in court. This person might observe the child in your home. CASAs do not work for CPS. They are independent.

Case Plan: The list of steps and goals proposed by CPS and ultimately ordered by the Court. A parent or a child, through counsel, can request modifications to the proposed case plan when needed. The list will include all of the steps for a parent to obtain custody of their child. The case plan will also include medical treatment for the child as well as psychological testing and therapy where appropriate. Also, the judge's instructions about the limits on visitation with parents, at least initially, will be written out.

Child Placing Agency: A private company authorized and regulated by the State. This agency may provide foster care and/or adoptive placements for children in foster care. The agency provides services to the participating placement family, including having a case manager assigned to the foster/adoptive placement in addition to the CPS case manager assigned to the case.

Child's Attorney: The child will be appointed an attorney to represent the child's interests. This attorney will tell the Court what the child wants and does not take direction from you. This attorney has a different goal from the GAL.

Clerk of Juvenile Court: This person works for the judge but cannot make decisions for the judge.

CPS Case Manager: Person employed by CPS to make referrals for the child, to track down putative fathers, to make monthly contact with the caregiver and the child. This person makes reports to the Court about compliance with the case plan, visits, and contacts with you.

CPS Investigator: This person investigates allegations of abuse. This role is different from CPS Case Manager.

CPS Supervisor: The person supervising your case manager. The CPS supervisor is involved in most decisions made about each case. If you can't find your case manager, the supervisor is the person to call.

CSEC Screening: CSEC = Commercially Sexually Exploited Child; In cases where a child has been living on the streets and/or reports gang association, a screening for CSEC may be conducted. A trained evaluator will interview a child regarding the circumstances around their life to determine if the child has been exposed to any indicators for and/or experiences of Human Sex Trafficking.

CSI: Community Support for Individuals. This service is for behavioral support, funded by Medicaid. The provider is usually an individual with a Masters Degree in Social Work. Behavioral support will be in the vein of therapy and behavior modification through appropriate methods. The service provider may meet with the child or adolescent in the home or at school. CSI is a very low level of intervention.

CCFA: Comprehensive Child and Family Assessment. This report will be based on interviews with family, friends, teachers (where appropriate), alternate caregivers, evaluating the parents' home, discussing the family's and child's history, and generally making recommendations from a social work perspective on how best to reunite the family.

Dependency Hearing: CPS and their attorney must prove at this hearing by clear and convincing evidence that the child needs to be in care of CPS while the parents work to remedy the problems of abuse or neglect of the child in the home.

Disposition Hearing: At this hearing, CPS will present a proposed case plan and the Court will order the parents and CPS to accomplish the goals of the case plan. Understand that some of the goals will be matters related to the child's health, education, and welfare. Caregivers should pay close attention to these goals. Be sure to ask questions if subjects are unclear.

Family Team Meeting: A meeting to discuss how to reunite the family. The parents, the child (depending on age), the CPS workers, CASA and Guardian ad litem will be included. Ideas for a case plan may also come from this meeting.

Guardian ad litem (GAL): Attorney appointed to look out for the child's best interests and make recommendations to the Court. These recommendations do not have to be what the child wants, only what that attorney believes are in the best interests of the child. This person might observe the child in your home.

IFI: Intensive Family Intervention, also known as Iffy. A service provided by Medicaid to children and adolescents. IFI provides in home/in school therapy, behavioral coaching, and parent support to children at risk for being hospitalized for mental health or behavior issues. IFI serves children at risk for hospitalization, who have recently been discharged from an out-of-community placement (hospital or group home), or for whom the intensive therapy, coaching and parent support are recommended to avoid an out-of-community placement. Initially, IFI will continue for 12 weeks. Service providers may request additional time if the services are showing signs of improvement. The service is provided by specialists and led by a licensed clinician. IFI is the highest level of community-based intervention available through Medicaid.

Judge: Attorney-appointed or elected who makes decisions in a case based on the law and the facts presented in Court. Enforces case plans, determines whether children go home.

Medical Evaluations: Each child who enters CPS custody will have a medical evaluation, which would also include dental evaluation.

Parent aide: A person who may supervise visits with your child, and who may provide transportation for the child-to-parent visits. This person might also provide parenting instruction.

Parents' Attorney: Either appointed to the parents or hired by the parents, this lawyer represents the parents' interests.

Post Termination Review: These hearings will continue to occur until the child is adopted. As long as the child remains in the legal custody of CPS, the Court will maintain a schedule of reviews to insure the child's welfare. The parents will not be part of these proceedings, as their rights have been terminated.

Preliminary Protective Hearing: This hearing may be referred to as a Preliminary Hearing or a 72-hour hearing. CPS must notify the parents of the time and place of this hearing. The hearing should be conducted within 72 hours of the child's being taken into CPS custody, though a deadline falling on a weekend or holiday will be considered to fall on the next business day. Any person interested in the child's welfare would be among those who may be present and may be heard on the issues in this hearing.

 The Court must determine if there is probable cause to keep the child in CPS custody based on evidence relating to abuse or neglect of the child. If there is such a ruling, the child will remain in care until the Dependency Hearing. Or, the Court could find that there is no probable cause and release the child back to the parents. Formerly called Shelter Care Hearing. First opportunity to raise temporary alternative placement, like fictive kin.

 Protective Order: This Order is from a judge requiring a parent to meet certain conditions before being released from DFCS/CPS supervision. Because this Order comes from the judge, failing to meet the conditions of the order could find a parent in contempt and/or result in a Dependency Case being opened and the child(ren) being removed from the household.

 PRTF: Psychiatric Residential Treatment Facility. To have a child or adult committed to a mental health facility, a doctor must make an application to ASO or their insurance provider. ASO Healthcare is a privacy agency charged with approving treatment plans for traditional Medicaid providers and with auditing agencies for financial and clinical practice.

 ASO evaluates the child/adult based on admission criteria. Approval by ASO does not mean automatic placement in a facility. There must be a proven record of a failure of community-based services to meet the child's needs. The exception is when a person is an imminent threat to themselves or others.

 Psychiatric Evaluation: During a DFCS/CPS case, an evaluation by a psychiatrist, a medical doctor focused on the brain and mental health, will usually be requested to determine if medication is necessary to treat some mental health diagnosis.

The psychiatric evaluation may be request for diagnosing mental health symptoms.

Psychological Evaluation: This report is a compilation of psychological testing conducted at the direction of a psychologist. These tests will include written scales (evaluation), verbal testing and observation. The psychological evaluation requires four steps. First, an appointment must be scheduled with the psychologist. Second, the patient must complete all testing. Third, an appointment to review the evaluation with the psychologist must be scheduled. Finally, attend appointment when the patient and any guardian will review the evaluation with the psychologist to learn the results of the testing. The psychologist will make recommendations for further treatment. These recommendations will become part of the case plan. If a parent or child or caregiver has questions about these recommendations, that appointment is the time to ask the questions.

Psychologist: A doctor with a Ph.D. or Psy.D. who may give written and verbal tests to you and your child. A psychologist may also provide therapy for you and/or your child. Someone hired by CPS as an outside contractor who provides service for a fee. A psychologist may also provide therapy for you and/or the child. Someone hired by CPS as an outside contractor who provides service for a fee. A psychologist may also ask to observe the child with the parent in a controlled setting as part of the parent's evaluation.

Removal Order: When CPS presents the Court with facts that support removing a child from a home. The order may initially be issued over the phone, but a written order including the Court's finding of facts must be filed with the Court.

Reviews: These periodic hearings provide the Judge an opportunity to cajole parents, scold CPS for falling short, praise parents for progress, tweak case plans when requested, and generally keep track of the case plan progress. Each judge has his or her own schedule for holding these review hearings; they occur sometimes every three months, sometimes every six months.

SAAG-Special Assistant Attorney General: The attorney who represents CPS. This person looks out for CPS's interests, which may or may not be the same as those of the caregiver.

Safety Plan: In some cases, CPS decides to work with parents to resolve issues before removing a child legally from a parent's care. The Safety Plan is an agreement between parents and CPS. Sometimes as a part of the Safety Plan, a child will be placed with a family member or friend as a caregiver resource. The caregiver resource must follow the Safety Plan, too.

Social worker: A social worker may give tests. A social worker can provide therapy for you. Someone hired by CPS as an outside contractor who provides service for a fee.

Staffing: A meeting where CPS talks about the progress of the case and what steps should be taken to accomplish reunification. CPS might include the SAAG, the Guardian ad litem, and the CASA. In some instances, the staffing might result in decisions about non-reunification and adoption options as well.

Termination of Parental Rights: When a parent fails to substantially complete a case plan, CPS files a Petition to Terminate Parental Rights. Termination is the final severing of parental rights and legal ties between parent and child. The Court will be cautious in proceeding to this point in the case. Understand that this process takes time. Attorneys will fight harder to avoid termination for parents. The termination may be set and continued a couple of times before the hearing is finally completed. Caregivers testify in these hearings about the current circumstances of the child. Be prepared to testify how the child is doing in school, who provides therapy, what if any medical conditions and medications the child may have.

<u>Visitation supervisor</u>: A person trained to observe parent visits, make notes about the visit, intervene if behaviors are not appropriate, and report to the CPS and the Court about visits.

Section Four

Record Keeping

Tracking your Case Plan

Case Plan Goal 1: _____

_____

Goal for whom: (circle one)   Parent   Child   CPS

Action required for Goal: _____

_____

____ Goal Accomplished (check off when completed)

Case Plan Goal 2: _____

_____

Goal for whom: (circle one)   Parent   Child   CPS

Action required for Goal: _____

_____

____ Goal Accomplished (check off when completed)

Case Plan Goal 3: _____

_____

Goal for whom: (circle one)   Parent   Child   CPS

Action required for Goal: _____

_____

____ Goal Accomplished (check off when completed)

Case Plan Goal 4: _____

_____

Goal for whom: (circle one) Parent   Child   CPS

Action required for Goal: _____

_____

____ Goal Accomplished (check off when completed)

Case Plan Goal 5: _____

_____

Goal for whom: (circle one) Parent   Child   CPS

Action required for Goal: _____

_____

____ Goal Accomplished (check off when completed)

Case Plan Goal 6: _____

_____

Goal for whom: (circle one) Parent   Child   CPS

Action required for Goal: _____

_____

____ Goal Accomplished (check off when completed)

Case Plan Goal 7: _____

_____

Goal for whom: (circle one) Parent   Child   CPS

Action required for Goal: _____

_____

_____ Goal Accomplished (check off when completed)

Case Plan Goal 8: _____

_____

Goal for whom: (circle one) Parent   Child   CPS

Action required for Goal: _____

_____

_____ Goal Accomplished (check off when completed)

Case Plan Goal 9: _____

_____

Goal for whom: (circle one) Parent   Child   CPS

Action required for Goal: _____

_____

_____ Goal Accomplished (check off when completed)

Case Plan Goal 10: _____

Goal for whom: (circle one)   Parent   Child   CPS

Action required for Goal: _____

_____

____ Goal Accomplished (check off when completed)

Names, Numbers, and Titles

Court Personnel

Name of Child's Attorney _____

Attorney Phone Number _____

Guardian ad Litem _____

    Guardian ad Litem's Phone Number _____

CASA Name _____

    CASA Phone Number _____

Judge's Name _____

    Court's Phone Number _____

DFCS Personnel

Case Manager _____

    Case Manager's Phone Number _____

Case Manager _____

    Case Manager's Phone Number _____

Case Manager _____

    Case Manager's Phone Number _____

Case Manager _____

Case Manager's Phone Number _____

Case Manager _____

Case Manager's Phone Number _____

Case Manager _____

Case Manager's Phone Number _____

Case Manager **Supervisor's** Name _____

Case Manager's Supervisor's Phone Number

_____

Treatment Providers

CCFA Evaluator _____

CCFA Evaluator's Phone Number _____

Therapist Name _____

Therapist's Phone Number _____

Parent Aide Name _____

Parent Aide's Phone Number _____

Visitation Supervisor _____

Visitation Supervisor's Phone Number _____

Child's Medical Doctor _____

Child's Medical Doctor's Phone Number _____

Child's Psychologist _____

    Child's Psychologist's Phone Number _____

Child's Therapist Name _____

    Child's Therapist's Phone Number _____

Care Coordinating Agency _____

Care Coordinator _____

    Care Coordinator's Phone Number: _____

School Contacts

Name of Child's School _____

    Principal's Name _____

    School Phone Number _____

    Teacher's Name _____

    Teacher's Email _____

    Teacher's Contact Phone Number _____

Contact Log

Date: _____ Time: _____

Contact: _____

Phone Number: _____

Notes: _____

_____

_____

Date: _____ Time: _____

Contact: _____

Phone Number: _____

Notes: _____

_____

_____

Date: _____ Time: _____

Contact: _____

Phone Number: _____

Notes: _____

_____

Date: _____ Time: _____

Contact: _____

Phone Number: _____

Notes:_____

_____

_____

Date: _____ Time: _____

Contact: _____

Phone Number: _____

Notes:_____

_____

_____

Date: _____ Time: _____

Contact: _____

Phone Number: _____

Notes:_____

_____

_____

Date: _____ Time: _____

Contact: _____

Phone Number: _____

Notes:_____

_____

_____

Date: _____ Time: _____

Contact: _____

Phone Number: _____

Notes:_____

_____

_____

Date: _____ Time: _____

Contact: _____

Phone Number: _____

Notes:_____

_____

_____

Date: _____ Time: _____

Contact: _____

Phone Number: _____

Notes:_____

_____

_____

Date: _____ Time: _____

Contact: _____

Phone Number: _____

Notes:_____

_____

_____

Date: _____ Time: _____

Contact: _____

Phone Number: _____

Notes:_____

_____

_____

Date: _____ Time: _____

Contact: _____

Phone Number: _____

Notes:_____

_____

_____

Date: _____ Time: _____

Contact: _____

Phone Number: _____

Notes:_____

_____

_____

Date: _____ Time: _____

Contact: _____

Phone Number: _____

Notes:_____

_____

_____

Date: _____ Time: _____

Contact: _____

Phone Number: _____

Notes:_____

_____

_____

Date: _____ Time: _____

Contact: _____

Phone Number: _____

Notes:_____

_____

_____

Date: _____ Time: _____

Contact: _____

Phone Number: _____

Notes:_____

_____

_____

Date: _____ Time: _____

Contact: _____

Phone Number: _____

Notes:_____

_____

_____

Date: _____ Time: _____

Contact: _____

Phone Number: _____

Notes:_____

_____

_____

Date: _____ Time: _____

Contact: _____

Phone Number: _____

Notes:_____

_____

_____

Date: _____ Time: _____

Contact: _____

Phone Number: _____

Notes:_____

_____

_____

Date: _____ Time: _____

Contact: _____

Phone Number: _____

Notes:_____

_____

_____

Date: _____ Time: _____

Contact: _____

Phone Number: _____

Notes:_____

_____

_____

Date: _____ Time: _____

Contact: _____

Phone Number: _____

Notes:_____

_____

_____

Date: _____ Time: _____

Contact: _____

Phone Number: _____

Notes:_____

_____

_____

Date: _____ Time: _____

Contact: _____

Phone Number: _____

Notes:_____

_____

_____

Date: _____ Time: _____

Contact: _____

Phone Number: _____

Notes:_____

_____

_____

Date: _____ Time: _____

Contact: _____

Phone Number: _____

Notes:_____

_____

_____

Date: _____ Time: _____

Contact: _____

Phone Number: _____

Notes:_____

_____

_____

Date: _____ Time: _____

Contact: _____

Phone Number: _____

Notes:_____

_____

_____

Date: _____ Time: _____

Contact: _____

Phone Number: _____

Notes:_____

_____

_____

Date: _____ Time: _____

Contact: _____

Phone Number: _____

Notes:_____

_____

_____

Date: _____ Time: _____

Contact: _____

Phone Number: _____

Notes: _____

_____

_____

Date: _____ Time: _____

Contact: _____

Phone Number: _____

Notes: _____

_____

_____

Date: _____ Time: _____

Contact: _____

Phone Number: _____

Notes: _____

_____

_____

Date: _____ Time: _____

Contact: _____

Phone Number: _____

Notes: _____

_____

_____

Date: _____ Time: _____

Contact: _____

Phone Number: _____

Notes: _____

_____

_____

Date: _____ Time: _____

Contact: _____

Phone Number: _____

Notes: _____

_____

_____

Date: _____ Time: _____

Contact: _____

Phone Number: _____

Notes:_____

_____

_____

Date: _____ Time: _____

Contact: _____

Phone Number: _____

Notes:_____

_____

_____

Date: _____ Time: _____

Contact: _____

Phone Number: _____

Notes:_____

_____

_____

Date: _____ Time: _____

Contact: _____

Phone Number: _____

Notes:_____

_____

_____

Date: _____ Time: _____

Contact: _____

Phone Number: _____

Notes:_____

_____

_____

Date: _____ Time: _____

Contact: _____

Phone Number: _____

Notes:_____

_____

_____

Date: _____ Time: _____

Contact: _____

Phone Number: _____

Notes:_____

_____

_____

Date: _____ Time: _____

Contact: _____

Phone Number: _____

Notes:_____

_____

_____

Date: _____ Time: _____

Contact: _____

Phone Number: _____

Notes:_____

_____

_____

Date: _____ Time: _____

Contact: _____

Phone Number: _____

Notes:_____

_____

_____

Date: _____ Time: _____

Contact: _____

Phone Number: _____

Notes:_____

_____

_____

Date: _____ Time: _____

Contact: _____

Phone Number: _____

Notes:_____

_____

_____

Date: _____ Time: _____

Contact: _____

Phone Number: _____

Notes: _____

_____

_____

Date: _____ Time: _____

Contact: _____

Phone Number: _____

Notes: _____

_____

_____

Date: _____ Time: _____

Contact: _____

Phone Number: _____

Notes: _____

_____

_____

Date: _____ Time: _____

Contact: _____

Phone Number: _____

Notes:_____

_____

_____

Date: _____ Time: _____

Contact: _____

Phone Number: _____

Notes:_____

_____

_____

Date: _____ Time: _____

Contact: _____

Phone Number: _____

Notes:_____

_____

_____

Date: _____ Time: _____

Contact: _____

Phone Number: _____

Notes:_____

_____

_____

Date: _____ Time: _____

Contact: _____

Phone Number: _____

Notes:_____

_____

_____

Date: _____ Time: _____

Contact: _____

Phone Number: _____

Notes:_____

_____

_____

Date: _____ Time: _____

Contact: _____

Phone Number: _____

Notes:_____

_____

_____

Date: _____ Time: _____

Contact: _____

Phone Number: _____

Notes:_____

_____

_____

Date: _____ Time: _____

Contact: _____

Phone Number: _____

Notes:_____

_____

_____

Date: _____ Time: _____

Contact: _____

Phone Number: _____

Notes:_____

_____

_____

Date: _____ Time: _____

Contact: _____

Phone Number: _____

Notes:_____

_____

_____

Date: _____ Time: _____

Contact: _____

Phone Number: _____

Notes:_____

_____

_____

Date: _____ Time: _____

Contact: _____

Phone Number: _____

Notes:_____

_____

_____

Date: _____ Time: _____

Contact: _____

Phone Number: _____

Notes:_____

_____

_____

Date: _____ Time: _____

Contact: _____

Phone Number: _____

Notes:_____

_____

_____

Date: _____ Time: _____

Contact: _____

Phone Number: _____

Notes:_____

_____

Date: _____ Time: _____

Contact: _____

Phone Number: _____

Notes:_____

_____

_____

Date: _____ Time: _____

Contact: _____

Phone Number: _____

Notes:_____

_____

_____

Date: _____ Time: _____

Contact: _____

Phone Number: _____

Notes:_____

_____

_____

Date: _____ Time: _____

Contact: _____

Phone Number: _____

Notes:_____

_____

_____

Date: _____ Time: _____

Contact: _____

Phone Number: _____

Notes:_____

_____

_____

Date: _____ Time: _____

Contact: _____

Phone Number: _____

Notes:_____

_____

_____

Date: _____ Time: _____

Contact: _____

Phone Number: _____

Notes:_____

_____

_____

Date: _____ Time: _____

Contact: _____

Phone Number: _____

Notes:_____

_____

_____

Date: _____ Time: _____

Contact: _____

Phone Number: _____

Notes:_____

_____

_____

Date: _____ Time: _____

Contact: _____

Phone Number: _____

Notes:_____

_____

_____

Date: _____ Time: _____

Contact: _____

Phone Number: _____

Notes:_____

_____

_____

Date: _____ Time: _____

Contact: _____

Phone Number: _____

Notes:_____

_____

_____

Date: _____ Time: _____

Contact: _____

Phone Number: _____

Notes:_____

_____

_____

Date: _____ Time: _____

Contact: _____

Phone Number: _____

Notes:_____

_____

_____

Date: _____ Time: _____

Contact: _____

Phone Number: _____

Notes:_____

_____

_____

Date: _____ Time: _____

Contact: _____

Phone Number: _____

Notes:_____

_____

_____

Date: _____ Time: _____

Contact: _____

Phone Number: _____

Notes:_____

_____

_____

Date: _____ Time: _____

Contact: _____

Phone Number: _____

Notes: _____

_____

_____

Date: _____ Time: _____

Contact: _____

Phone Number: _____

Notes: _____

_____

_____

Date: _____ Time: _____

Contact: _____

Phone Number: _____

Notes: _____

_____

_____

Date: _____ Time: _____

Contact: _____

Phone Number: _____

Notes:_____

_____

_____

Date: _____ Time: _____

Contact: _____

Phone Number: _____

Notes:_____

_____

_____

Date: _____ Time: _____

Contact: _____

Phone Number: _____

Notes:_____

_____

_____

Date: _____ Time: _____

Contact: _____

Phone Number: _____

Notes:_____

_____

_____

Date: _____ Time: _____

Contact: _____

Phone Number: _____

Notes:_____

_____

_____

Date: _____ Time: _____

Contact: _____

Phone Number: _____

Notes:_____

_____

_____

Court Dates

Below you will find spaces for the re-setting of some early court dates: many times, a case has to be rescheduled for a myriad of reasons. If the continuance causes concern for the child, please notify the CASA and/or Guardian ad Litem.

Note that some courts use Citizen Review Panels instead of frequent reviews in front of the Judge. Feel free to modify the interim reviews (3, 9, 15, 21) to reflect Citizen Review Panel.

Preliminary Protective Hearing: _____

Reset of P.P. Hearing: _____

Dependency Hearing: _____

Reset of Dependency Hearing: _____

Disposition Hearing: _____

Reset of Disposition Hearing: _____

3 month Review: _____

6 month Review: _____

9 month Review: _____

12 month Review: _____

15 month Review: _____

18 month Review: _____

21 month Review: _____

24 month Review: _____

Termination Hearing: _____

Reset of Termination Hearing: _____

www.ingramcontent.com/pod-product-compliance
Lightning Source LLC
Chambersburg PA
CBHW071414210526
45465CB00001B/379